Inner Talk
for a
Love that Works

BY DR. SUSAN JEFFERS

Books

Feel the Fear and Do It Anyway
Opening Our Hearts to Men
Dare to Connect
Inner Talk for a Confident Day
Inner Talk for a Love that Works
Inner Talk for Peace of Mind
The Journey from Lost to Found

Audios

Feel the Fear and Do It Anyway
A Fearbusting Workshop
The Art of Fearbusting
Opening Our Hearts to Each Other
Flirting from the Heart
Inner Talk for a Confident Day
Inner Talk for a Love that Works
Inner Talk for Peace of Mind
Opening Our Hearts to Men
Dare to Connect

Inner Talk *for a* Love that Works

SUSAN JEFFERS, Ph.D.

Hay House, Inc.
Carson, CA

INNER TALK FOR A LOVE THAT WORKS
by Susan Jeffers, Ph.D.

Copyright © 1992 by Susan Jeffers, Ph.D.

The author of this book does not dispense medical advice nor prescribe the use of any technique as a form of treatment for physical or medical problems without the advice of a physician, either directly or indirectly. The intent of the author is only to offer information of a general nature to help you in your quest for mental fitness. In the event you use any of the information in this book for yourself, which is your constitutional right, the author and the publisher assume no responsibility for your actions.

Library of Congress Cataloging-in-Publication Data

Jeffers, Susan J.
    Inner talk for a love that works / by Susan Jeffers.
        p.   cm.
    ISBN 1-56170-050-9 : $5:00 (tradepaper)
    1. Love—Problems, exercises, etc.   2. Affirmations.
  3. Self-talk. I. Title.
BF575.L8J45   1992
152.4'1—dc20   92-15717
                                     CIP

Library of Congress Catalog Card No. 92-15717
ISBN: 1-56170-049-5

Internal design by David Butler
Typesetting by Freedmen's Organization, Los Angeles, CA 90004
93 94 95 96 97 10 9 8 7 6 5 4 3 2
First Printing, June 1992
Second Printing, October 1993

Published and Distributed in the United States by:
Hay House, Inc.
P. O. Box 6204
Carson, CA 90749-6204

Printed in the United States of America
on Recycled Paper

DEDICATION

To the Miracles—
That Love Brings into our Lives

PREFACE

It is my joy to bring to you some powerful Inner Talk that will help you take charge of Love. The words you are now going to read are about creating greater closeness with that special person in your life. If you are not in a romantic relationship, apply the messages to someone close to you—a friend, a parent, a child, a co-worker. It's good practice. After all, love is love . . . with whomever we find it!

The aim of these positive messages is to help replace any negative thoughts you may hold about your past, present or future relationships with the empowering thoughts of the Higher Self, the best of who you are. As you do, you will understand what it truly means to honor yourself . . . and others.

Remember, you do not have to believe these words for them to have a healing effect. Trust that, at some level, their message is being heard.

Ideally, this book should be read daily for at least one month . . . or until the words become automatic in your thinking. As you read, intermittently take a deep breath to allow the body to relax into the warming energy that is being created. When you can, say the words out loud. If you have the audiotape, listen to it whenever you can, such as when you are lying in bed, exercising or dressing. When you hear, speak and read these positive thoughts, the impact is enhanced. You can also carry the book with you throughout the day to be used whenever you want to remind yourself what a "Higher" love looks like.

As you read *Inner Talk for a Love that Works* over and over again, you will slowly learn how to live into a life filled with love.

From my Higher Self to yours,

Susan Jeffers

Inner Talk for a Love that Works

I am now ready to create a love that works . . . a love that comes from the highest part of who I am. I am now ready to create the caring environment in which this Higher Love can take seed and bloom. I take a deep breath and I feel my loving energy grow.

To guide me on this path of love with the special person now in my life . . . or with someone I will one day meet . . . I affirm the following words from the best of who I am . . .

I am healing the inner hurts that stop me from loving myself and loving you.

I am letting go of negative emotions that keep me separated from love.

I am letting go of the need to blame . . . myself or you.

I am transforming my neediness into authentic caring.

I am taking action to create a rich and nourishing life.

I am surrounding myself with people who bring me joy.

I am learning to trust that I am a person of worth.

I am pulling up the great power that resides within me.

I am opening my heart to love.

I am opening my heart to love.

I am opening my heart to love.

I now take the time to look at those emotions that separate me from love. I look first at any anger I may be holding toward people in my life . . . past or present. I release them of all blame knowing that blame is a powerless act.

Instead I accept my anger as a sign that it is now time for me to take control of my actions and reactions in life. To channel my anger into a positive tool of self-discovery and self-healing, I affirm the following words that come from the Power Within . . .

I am sculpting my life the way I want it to be.

I have choice in my life.

I am now taking action.

I have nothing to fear.

I am reclaiming my power.

With an open heart, I move out of the way of those who try to hurt me.

I see their inner pain and lovingly let them go.

I am drawing nourishing people into my life.

*I am creating a life filled
with love.*

*I am creating a life filled
with love.*

*I am creating a life filled
with love.*

As I release others from blame, I am careful not to blame myself. I know that all my experiences are a source of growth and learning.

No matter what has happened in my life,
I lovingly affirm the following . . .

There are no mistakes . . . only opportunities for growth.

I stand tall and take responsibility for my life.

I am worthy of dignity and love.

I am a lover-in-training and I am learning my lessons well.

I am learning something valuable from all life experiences.

I follow my Inner Light that leads the way to love.

I trust who I am.

I trust who I am.

I trust who I am.

I am now creating a safe space for greater intimacy to occur. I understand that we are both doing the very best that we can to share our truth with one another.

To help keep the feeling of closeness alive, I affirm the following . . .

I am your friend.

I am on your side.

I am sending you thoughts of love.

I listen to and I hear what you have to say.

I open my heart to receive.

I accept all your actions as your desire to be loved.

I see the beauty within you.

I am letting in your love.

I am letting in your love.

I am letting in your love.

I pick up the mirror and look at my need to be right . . . my need to always have the last word. I now know I am good enough. I love and respect all of who I am.

There is nothing I have to prove . . . to you or to me. With confidence in myself, I lovingly affirm the following . . .

I open up to hear what you have to say.

I respect your point of view as I respect my own.

I see in you much of what I need to learn.

From the level of the Soul, we are One.

I love you.

I love you.

I love you.

I now learn the meaning of trust. I know that the only thing I can safely trust is my ability to handle whatever you say or do to me.

We are both human and cannot predict the future. When I fully trust myself, the fear goes away, and what's left is the love.

I trust who I am.

I handle whatever happens in my life.

I am cutting the cord of dependency.

My self-esteem is growing every day.

I am creating a beautiful life.

I trust the future.

There's always more.

I am strong and I am whole.

I am strong and I am whole.

I am strong and I am whole.

I now release all my negative judgments. I let go of my anger and fear and appreciate what is truly wonderful about you. I am learning how to take as I acknowledge and appreciate what you bring into my life . . . no matter how big . . . no matter how small.

I feel surrounded by abundance as I affirm the following words from my Higher Self . . .

I thank you for the many things you do
for me.

I thank you for your many acts of
kindness.

I thank you for sharing so many wonderful moments.

I thank you for the times you think
about me.

I thank you for what I learn about myself
through you.

I thank you for listening and loving and
caressing and cajoling and laughing
and trying and hoping and caring and
being and doing and buying and support-
ing and sharing and helping and
nurturing and protecting and walking
the walk and talking the talk.

I thank you for being a part of my life.

Thank You.

Thank You.

Thank You.

In order to truly love you, it is essential that I learn to love who I am. To love who I am means to know in my mind, to feel in my heart, and to reflect into this world my Inner Beauty, my Inner Strength, and my Inner Light.

I pick up the mirror and focus on all the beauty that lies within my Body, Mind and Soul. In my actions and in my words, I lovingly remind myself that at the level of my Highest Self . . .

I am filled with a vibrant Living Force.

I am capable and whole.

I am a responsible person.

I am powerful and I am loving.

I am a pleasure to know.

I am filled with beauty, strength and light.

My life makes a difference.

I touch the world wherever I go.

I have so much to give.

I hold my head up high.

I deserve love.

I love who I am.

I love who I am.

I love who I am.

As I learn to love who I am, I support you
in learning to love who you are.

I always let you know through my actions and my words that at the level of your Highest Self . . .

You are filled with a vibrant Living Force.

You are capable and whole.

You are a responsible person.

You are powerful and you are loving.

You are a pleasure to know.

You are filled with beauty, strength and light.

Your life makes a difference.

You touch the world wherever you go.

You have so much to give.

You can hold your head up high.

You deserve love.

I love who you are.

I love who you are.

I love who you are.

I let go of fairy tale expectations that set me up for disappointment. The only expectation I have of this relationship—or any relationship, whether it lasts one week, twenty-five years, or until death do us part—is that I will learn more about opening my heart and becoming a more loving person.

I am a Lover-in-Training. To create a love that works requires awareness and practice. I commit to taking those steps that guide me toward a Higher Love. To keep me on the path, I affirm the following . . .

My being a loving person depends only
on me.

I am creating an inner energy of love
that touches everyone around me.

I am warming the world with my love.

My life makes a difference.

The love in my life begins with me.

I love who I am.

I am pulling up the Great Power
within me.

I am opening my heart to love.

I am opening my heart to love.

I am opening my heart to love.

To create a Higher Love, I know I must be a lover of humanity. The more I become a "lover" in the world outside my relationship, the more I can be a lover inside my relationship.

I remind myself over and over again, I am needed to bring more love into this world. There are so many people who would welcome my love.

I am reaching out to those around me.

I am inviting others into my life.

My eyes say, ''Welcome.''

My smile says, ''I would like to know you
better.''

My heart says, ''I care.''

I embrace the world like a lover!

I embrace the world like a lover!

I embrace the world like a lover!

I begin each day by asking myself, "If I were really important in this home, this community, and this world, what would I be doing? And I do it . . . one step at a time.

With each step that I take, I live into the full awareness of my Higher Purpose in life . . .

My Higher Purpose is to ease someone's pain.

My Higher Purpose is to care.

My Higher Purpose is to share.

My Higher Purpose is to give.

My Higher Purpose is to have compassion.

My Higher Purpose is to project light wherever I go.

I warm the world with my love.

I warm the world with my love.

I warm the world with my love.

On the following pages, write those Inner Talk messages that speak to you most powerfully at this moment in your life. Or, begin creating your own Inner Talk for a Love that Works.

INNER TALK FOR A LOVE THAT WORKS

INNER TALK FOR A LOVE THAT WORKS

INNER TALK FOR A LOVE THAT WORKS

INNER TALK FOR A LOVE THAT WORKS